LOVE D CODE

UNLOCKING THE SECRETS OF GIVERS AND SEEKERS

DILIP CHAKRAVARTHY

Made with ♥ on the Notion Press Platform
www.notionpress.com

"Dedicated to my future partner, who's probably lost somewhere in the algorithm of life.

Until then, I'm single, thriving, and writing books."

Contents

Foreword

Warning:

If you're single, happily living your best life, and have absolutely zero interest in love or relationships, this book is probably not for you. But hey, no worries! You can gift it to a friend in need of some love advice, or just stash it away until you feel like diving into the world of romance—because who knows? One day, even the happiest of singles might need a little love story in their life.

ONE

INTRODUCTION:

"Love is the ultimate story we write, where every relationship becomes a chapter reflecting who we are and who we aspire to be."

A Personal Journey into the Dynamics of Love

Over the years, I have had the privilege of being approached by countless individuals seeking advice on their relationships. As a cinematographer, I've spent much of my life shaping stories—creating characters, weaving emotions, and examining the complexities of human interaction. While I could effortlessly piece together the perfect narrative on screen, I often found myself grappling with deeper questions about the nature of relationships in real life. What makes a relationship thrive? Why do some connections withstand the test of time while others crumble under pressure? These questions consumed my curiosity, leading me on a journey that I never expected to take.

Despite coming from a commerce background and earning my master's degree in M.Com, my fascination with human psychology always remained a guiding force. I immersed myself in studying human behavior, delving into books and research papers on the subject. Case studies became my playground, and I often found myself creating stories based on the insights I uncovered. The more I read, the more I realized that relationships were not just about emotions but about patterns, conditioning, and subconscious influences that shape our interactions.

This exploration into the psychological aspects of relationships gradually turned into an obsession. I found myself questioning why people crave love so deeply and what they truly mean when they say, "I love you." What drives this yearning for connection, and why does the meaning of love often evolve over time? I began to notice patterns—how certain experiences, fears, and desires influence the way people approach relationships. I wanted to decode these mysteries, to understand what lies beneath the surface of romantic connections.

My research led me to understand that love is far more than just an emotion—it is a complex interplay of biology, psychology, and social dynamics. Hormones like dopamine and oxytocin play a crucial role in creating feelings of attachment and euphoria, while past experiences and upbringing shape how we interpret and express love. I was fascinated by how these elements interact to create the tapestry of emotions we experience in relationships.

One of the most intriguing discoveries during my studies was how relationships often act as mirrors, reflecting our insecurities, fears, and aspirations. I found myself drawn to the idea that relationships are not just about two people coming together but about how each person projects their inner world onto the other. This realization compelled me to explore further. I wanted to know why some people fall in love quickly while others remain guarded, and why some relationships feel effortless while others require constant work.

As someone who has always been a storyteller, I couldn't help but weave these insights into narratives. I created countless stories inspired by real-life scenarios and hypothetical situations, using them to dissect emotions and motivations. These stories allowed me to step into the shoes of different characters, experiencing their triumphs and struggles as they navigated love and loss.

Over time, I began to notice a recurring theme—love is not static. It changes, evolves, and sometimes even fades. But what causes this shift? Is it external circumstances, internal growth, or a combination of both? I realized that relationships often mirror the human condition—a constant state of flux driven by the need for growth and fulfillment. This understanding deepened my passion for exploring love's many dimensions.

The questions I grappled with—why people want love, how they define it, and what causes its transformation—are the foundation of this book. My aim is not to provide definitive answers but to offer insights that encourage readers to reflect on their own relationships. Through personal anecdotes, psychological studies, and thought-provoking stories, I hope to shed light on the invisible forces that shape our connections.

This book is a culmination of my years of research, introspection, and storytelling. It is an attempt to unravel the mysteries of love and relationships while acknowledging their inherent complexity. Whether you are someone seeking answers, navigating a difficult relationship, or simply curious about the psychology of love, this book is for you.

In the chapters that follow, we will explore the different facets of relationships—from the initial spark of attraction to the challenges of maintaining intimacy over time. We will examine the roles of communication, trust, and vulnerability, as well as the impact of past experiences and societal expectations. Through this journey, my hope is to empower readers to view love not as a destination but as a continuous process of growth, discovery, and connection.

So let us embark on this exploration together—one that promises to decode the mysteries of love and relationships, offering new perspectives and deeper understanding along the way.

The Concept of Givers and Seekers

I am not a trained psychiatrist, but I've always had an intrinsic curiosity about human behavior. As I began diving into psychology and reflecting on my personal observations, I began to notice patterns emerging in the relationships around me. Whether it was my friends, family, or acquaintances, it became increasingly clear that people in relationships often fall into one of two categories:

Givers and Seekers. The roles of Givers and Seekers seemed to play a significant role in determining the success or failure of relationships. Through these patterns, I started to uncover a deeper understanding of what makes love work—and why it falters.

Givers are those who naturally prioritize the needs and happiness of their partners. They derive joy from offering support, care, and affection, often placing their partner's well-being above their own. They find fulfillment in nurturing the relationship and often go to great lengths to maintain harmony. However, this tendency can sometimes lead to burnout or feelings of being taken for granted if their efforts are not reciprocated.

Seekers, on the other hand, approach relationships with a focus on their own emotional needs and desires. They often seek validation, attention, and reassurance from their partners. This is not necessarily a negative trait; in fact, Seekers can bring passion, excitement, and a strong sense of purpose to a relationship. However, if their needs become overwhelming or unbalanced, it can create tension and dependency.

What fascinated me most was how these roles are not fixed. People can shift between being Givers and Seekers depending on the dynamics of the relationship and their personal growth. For instance, someone who starts as a Seeker may evolve into a Giver after experiencing emotional security, while a Giver may adopt Seeker tendencies if they feel neglected.

This fluidity added another layer of complexity to my exploration. It highlighted the importance of balance and mutual understanding in relationships. When both partners are attuned to each other's needs and willing to adapt, the relationship thrives. But when one partner remains stuck in a single role, it can lead to frustration, resentment, and eventual breakdown.

Through my research and observations, I realized that identifying these roles early on can help couples address potential challenges before they escalate. By fostering open communication and empathy, partners can create a more harmonious and fulfilling connection.

In the next chapters, we will delve deeper into these roles, exploring how they manifest in different types of relationships and how recognizing them can lead to healthier dynamics. We will also discuss strategies for maintaining balance, addressing imbalances, and cultivating lasting love.

The Purpose of Understanding Relationship Patterns

This exploration into human behavior, combined with years of personal interactions and professional insights, led me to a powerful realization: the foundation of most relationships is built on whether someone is a Giver or a Seeker. Understanding these roles is key to building sustainable, meaningful connections. I began to see how the Giver-Seeker dynamic affected relationships—how a Giver's selflessness can nurture a connection, and how a Seeker's desires can create imbalance if not understood or managed properly.

By recognizing these patterns, individuals can gain clarity about their own behaviors and emotional needs. Givers can learn to set healthy boundaries, ensuring that their generosity doesn't lead to exhaustion. Seekers can develop self-awareness, discovering ways to fulfill their emotional needs without overwhelming their partners. My hope for this book is that by recognizing whether you are a Giver or a Seeker, you'll have the tools to create better, more fulfilling relationships—relationships that thrive on balance, mutual respect, and genuine connection.

Through this lens, we will explore practical strategies for identifying these roles, fostering communication, and addressing imbalances before they lead to breakdowns. The goal is not to label people but to provide insights that encourage growth and deeper understanding. With this foundation, readers will be equipped to transform their relationships into sources of strength, joy, and emotional growth.

Why This Book Matters for Lasting Love

The purpose of this book is not just to explain the roles of Givers and Seekers, but to provide a deeper understanding of the forces at play in love and relationships. Through my years of research, observation, and conversations with those seeking advice, I have uncovered patterns that reveal why relationships work or don't. By understanding these dynamics, you will be equipped to navigate your own love life more effectively.

The insights shared here are not merely theoretical; they come from years of personal experience, research, and the real stories of people seeking advice on love. This book aims to bridge the gap between theory and practice, providing actionable strategies that readers can apply to their own relationships.

Though I am not a psychologist by training, my profession as a cinematographer has allowed me to view human connections through a unique lens—one that combines the science of human interaction with the art of storytelling. Through this book, I invite you to explore love and relationships through the lens of the Giver and Seeker dynamic and uncover new ways to approach your connections, ensuring that they are not only meaningful but also lasting.

TWO

CHAPTER 1: UNDERSTANDING THE GIVER

"The heart of a Giver beats for others, but it must also learn to beat for itself."

Who is a Giver?

In the world of relationships, a "Giver" refers to someone who consistently invests in others, prioritizing their partner's needs, desires, and well-being over their own. Givers thrive on creating harmony, connection, and peace through acts of love, care, and devotion. For them, giving is not merely about material offerings; it encompasses time, empathy, emotional support, and attention. Their fulfillment stems from seeing their partner happy and content, often carrying out their actions without expecting anything in return.

The Psychology of a Giver

The mindset of a Giver is deeply rooted in empathy and altruism. Many Givers form strong emotional connections to the happiness and well-being of those around them. For some, this tendency emerges from early experiences in childhood—perhaps growing up in caregiving roles or where validation came from acts of service.

Psychologically, Givers are often highly intuitive and emotionally sensitive. They can easily detect the moods and needs of others, making them natural caretakers. However, this sensitivity also creates a tendency to avoid conflict, as they prioritize harmony over confrontation, even at their own expense.

For many Givers, their sense of identity and self-worth is intertwined with their ability to nurture and support others. This can lead them to associate love and approval with how much they give. Beyond love, the act of giving provides them with a sense of purpose and belonging—a belief that their value lies in their ability to uplift others.

How to Identify a Giver

Givers can often be recognized through their consistent actions and behaviors. They are the ones who:

Remember small details about their partner's likes, dislikes, and needs.

Go out of their way to provide comfort and support without being asked.

Offer words of encouragement and listen attentively during difficult times.

Show patience, even when their own needs are overlooked.

Frequently prioritize their partner's happiness over their own.

Examples of Givers in Action

Example 1: A Giver may wake up early to prepare their partner's favorite breakfast, even when they are tired, simply to brighten their partner's day.

Example 2: In a disagreement, a Giver might apologize first—not because they were wrong but because they value harmony over proving a point.

Example 3: A Giver may organize surprises or thoughtful gestures to celebrate their partner's accomplishments, showing appreciation and admiration.

Givers create warmth and stability in relationships, but it's essential to understand their patterns and tendencies to fully appreciate their role in love and connection.

The Selfless Nature of Givers in Relationships

Givers are inherently selfless, focusing on their partner's happiness and well-being. Their strength lies in their ability to give consistently and unconditionally, often fostering trust, respect, and emotional security in their relationships. However, this selflessness can sometimes lead to challenges, particularly if their efforts go unacknowledged or if they give at the expense of their own needs.

Key Characteristics of a Giver

Selflessness: Givers find joy in prioritizing their partner's happiness, often going out of their way to provide support—whether emotional, physical, or mental.

Nurturing: Givers naturally create a safe and caring environment, offering encouragement and emotional stability to their partners.

Emotional Availability: One of their defining traits is their ability to be emotionally present. Givers listen deeply and respond empathetically, fostering unbreakable emotional connections.

The Strength of Givers: Building Lasting Bonds

Givers excel at creating relationships rooted in trust, empathy, and mutual respect. Their genuine care and selfless actions form the foundation of love and loyalty. Unlike transactional relationships, which are driven by expectations, Giver-led connections thrive on shared emotional investment.

By consistently meeting their partner's needs—whether emotional, mental, or physical—Givers establish a lasting sense of security and comfort. This dynamic often becomes the bedrock of strong and enduring relationships.

Real-Life Examples: A Giver's Impact on Relationships

Aarav and Anika: Aarav, raised with a deep understanding of selflessness, met Anika, an independent woman hesitant to trust others. Aarav's small, consistent acts of kindness—checking on her well-being, helping with her challenges, and offering unconditional support—eventually helped Anika build trust. Over time, his emotional availability created a safe space for Anika to open up, leading to a deep, lasting connection.

Rhea and Karan: Rhea, a career-driven woman raised to hide her vulnerabilities, found herself drawn to Karan, a patient and emotionally available Giver. Through his unwavering support and nurturing nature, Karan helped Rhea feel safe enough to embrace her true self. This transformation taught Rhea the value of trust and emotional interdependence.

Challenges Faced by Givers

While Givers bring immense value to relationships, their selflessness can sometimes create challenges. Over-giving, for instance, may lead to emotional burnout or feelings of being taken for granted. Givers may also struggle to set boundaries, fearing that doing so could disrupt the harmony they strive to maintain.

Additionally, Givers may unintentionally enable dependency in their partners, especially if their giving is one-sided or unreciprocated. Recognizing these challenges is essential for Givers to maintain their well-being and ensure their relationships remain balanced and fulfilling.

Balancing the Giver's Role in Relationships

For Givers, maintaining balance is key to sustaining healthy relationships. Here are some strategies to help:

Set Boundaries: Learn to say "no" when needed, and prioritize your own well-being. Remember, self-care is not selfish.

Communicate Needs: Express your own desires and expectations clearly. Open communication fosters mutual understanding.

Encourage Reciprocity: Allow your partner to contribute to the relationship. Accepting support strengthens bonds and prevents imbalance.

Practice Self-Reflection: Regularly assess whether your giving is motivated by love or a fear of rejection. Adjust accordingly to ensure your actions align with your well-being.

Conclusion

Givers play a vital role in fostering trust, stability, and love in relationships. Their selflessness and emotional availability create bonds that stand the test of time. However, to maintain balance and prevent burnout, Givers must also nurture themselves and encourage reciprocity from their partners. By doing so, they can continue to give generously while building relationships that are not only enduring but also deeply fulfilling.

THREE

Chapter 2: Understanding the Seeker

"A Seeker searches outside for fulfilment, but the truest answers lie within."

Who is a Seeker?

A Seeker is someone driven by a persistent search for something external to fill an internal void. This need often revolves around love, attention, admiration, or material satisfaction. Seekers may not always recognize their quest, but their behaviours, relationships, and actions often reveal this underlying desire. While their pursuit of validation and fulfilment can bring passion and energy to relationships, it can also create challenges if not understood or balanced.

The Psychology of a Seeker

The mindset of a Seeker is shaped by an inherent need for validation, security, or fulfilment. Many Seekers are motivated by a desire to feel appreciated, admired, or emotionally complete. Their focus tends to be outward, looking to others to meet their emotional or material needs. This orientation often stems from insecurities, past experiences, or a fear of being alone or unloved.

Psychologically, Seekers may display traits of ambition and determination but often struggle with feelings of inadequacy when their expectations aren't met. Their emotional patterns frequently include a constant craving for reassurance or acknowledgment, which drives their pursuit of love and attention. For Seekers, external validation often becomes the measure of their self-worth, creating a cycle of emotional highs and lows based on the responses they receive from others.

This reliance on external affirmation can lead to challenges, especially in relationships. While Seekers may experience joy and satisfaction when their needs are met, they can feel anxious, insecure, or unfulfilled when they perceive a lack of attention or acknowledgment.

How to Identify a Seeker

A Seeker's behaviours and patterns often reveal their underlying needs. Common characteristics include:

Seeking compliments and words of affirmation frequently.

Feeling anxious or insecure when they don't receive attention.

Focusing on achieving external goals, such as wealth or social status, to feel validated.

Testing their partner's commitment through questions or behaviors.

Displaying excitement and enthusiasm in the early stages of a relationship but struggling to maintain emotional stability over time.

Examples of Seekers in Action

Example 1: A Seeker may frequently ask their partner whether they love them, seeking reassurance even after receiving prior affirmations.

Example 2: In social situations, a Seeker might go out of their way to dress or behave in ways that attract attention and admiration from others.

Example 3: A Seeker might feel disappointed or distant if their partner forgets to compliment them, interpreting it as a lack of love or appreciation.

While these tendencies can create challenges, understanding the motivations behind a Seeker's behaviours can foster greater empathy and connection in relationships.

The Emotional and Material Fulfilment of Seekers

Desire for Love: Seekers deeply crave love and emotional connection. They often believe that external love can fill their inner void, but they may struggle to offer the same in return. This can lead to unbalanced relationships, where Seekers feel empty despite receiving love.

Need for Attention: Attention and praise are critical for Seekers to feel validated. When ignored or unnoticed, they may experience insecurity or anxiety, straining their relationships as their partners feel overwhelmed by constant demands for reassurance.

Material Fulfilment: Beyond emotional needs, some Seekers prioritize material stability, such as financial support or status. While seeking security is natural, an overemphasis on material aspects can diminish the importance of emotional bonds and personal growth.

Why Seekers Need Givers in Relationships

Seekers are naturally drawn to Givers, who provide the emotional support and validation they seek. Givers' nurturing and selfless nature helps fulfil a Seeker's need for attention and reassurance, creating an initial sense of harmony. However, for these relationships to thrive, reciprocity is essential. Without mutual exchange, the Seeker's constant need for affirmation can drain the Giver, leading to resentment and imbalance.

To sustain a fulfilling relationship, Seekers must realize that love requires both giving and receiving. Emotional support, appreciation, and care must flow in both directions to maintain harmony. The Seeker's journey involves looking inward to address their own needs while learning the value of giving selflessly.

The Journey Toward Balance

For Seekers to thrive in relationships, self-awareness and growth are crucial. By reflecting on their motivations and learning to fulfil their emotional needs internally, Seekers can cultivate healthier dynamics. Practical steps for Seekers include:

Practice Self-Awareness: Reflect on the motivations behind your actions and behaviors. Are they driven by fear, insecurity, or a genuine desire to connect?

Develop Emotional Independence: Work on fulfilling your own emotional needs through self-care, personal growth, and hobbies.

Focus on Giving: Shift the focus from receiving to giving. Small acts of kindness and support can strengthen bonds and create mutual respect.

Communicate Openly: Express your needs and fears honestly, creating an opportunity for understanding and empathy in your relationship.

Real-Life Examples: A Seeker's Journey and Challenges

Neha's Story: Neha's relentless search for love left her feeling empty despite being with a selfless partner, Rohit. Over time, she realized her inability to reciprocate emotionally was draining their relationship. This painful epiphany marked the beginning of her journey toward understanding that love must flow both ways. Through self-reflection and counseling, Neha learned to appreciate Rohit's efforts and began contributing emotionally to their bond.

Siddharth's Story: Siddharth viewed relationships as transactional, offering little but expecting much. His emotional imbalance strained his bond with Priya, a nurturing Giver. When their relationship faltered, Siddharth recognized that love requires mutual investment and emotional reciprocity. This realization pushed him to change his approach, gradually learning to support Priya and value her contributions.

Challenges for Seekers in Relationships

While Seekers bring passion and energy to relationships, their patterns can create challenges if left unchecked. Over-reliance on external validation may lead to:

Emotional Imbalance: Placing excessive pressure on their partner to meet all their needs.

Resentment in Partners: Constantly seeking affirmation without giving back can lead to frustration and fatigue in the relationship.

Missed Growth Opportunities: A focus on external fulfillment may prevent Seekers from addressing internal insecurities and achieving personal growth.

The Path Forward for Seekers

By embracing personal growth and cultivating a balance between giving and receiving, Seekers can create fulfilling and enduring relationships. Developing emotional independence, practicing empathy, and nurturing their partners are key steps toward healthier dynamics.

Seekers have the potential to transform their relationships by recognizing their own worth, contributing meaningfully, and fostering mutual respect. In doing so, they not only enrich their connections but also find the inner fulfilment they seek.

FOUR

CHAPTER 3: GIVER + GIVER = THE PERFECT MATCH

"When two Givers unite, they create a harmony that echoes the deepest truths of love."

Why Two Givers Create Harmony and Balance

In a Giver + Giver relationship, harmony and balance naturally emerge because both partners share fundamental values—selflessness, emotional availability, and a deep desire to nurture others. These shared qualities create an environment where love flows freely, and mutual respect thrives.

Unlike relationships where one partner may feel the strain of always giving, a Giver + Giver partnership forms a natural equilibrium. Each person is equally committed to the other's happiness and well-being, leading to a bond built on appreciation and understanding. Instead of focusing on receiving, both partners prioritize building each other up, deriving immense joy from seeing the other succeed.

Though seemingly ideal, even Giver + Giver relationships require effort. Mutual respect for emotional needs and a commitment to self-care are crucial. Only by nurturing themselves can both partners sustain the love and giving that define their bond.

The Psychological Foundation of Giver + Giver Relationships

The success of Giver + Giver relationships can be explained through the psychological principles of altruism, attachment theory, and positive reinforcement.

Altruism and Emotional Fulfillment Psychologists define altruism as selfless concern for the well-being of others, and research has shown that acts of giving release oxytocin, the "love hormone." Oxytocin strengthens emotional bonds, creating feelings of trust and intimacy. When both partners exhibit high levels of altruism, the relationship becomes a source of emotional security and happiness.

Attachment Theory According to attachment theory, secure attachment styles develop when individuals feel safe, valued, and supported. Giver + Giver relationships mirror secure attachments, where both partners feel deeply cared for and emotionally available. Such connections minimize anxiety and insecurity, allowing the relationship to flourish.

Positive Reinforcement and Reciprocity The theory of positive reinforcement suggests that repeated acts of kindness and appreciation reinforce behaviors, encouraging even more giving. Giver + Giver couples naturally reinforce each other's generosity, creating a continuous cycle of mutual care and affection.

The Power of Reciprocity in Giver + Giver Relationships

Reciprocity in these relationships transcends the transactional exchange of gifts or favors. It revolves around emotional reciprocity, where acts of kindness and care are met with equal warmth and support. This cycle of mutual giving strengthens their connection, fostering a love that is profound and enduring.

For Givers, love isn't about keeping score. Instead, it's about creating a safe space for both partners to flourish. When one partner faces challenges or exhaustion, the other steps in with unwavering support, ensuring that the balance of giving remains intact.

How Giver + Giver Relationships Handle Issues

Giver + Giver relationships have a lower likelihood of conflict due to their shared values of empathy, understanding, and emotional availability. When issues arise, these couples approach them with cooperation rather than confrontation.

Active Listening and Empathy

Both partners prioritize listening to each other's concerns without judgment. This empathetic approach allows them to understand the root cause of the issue rather than reacting impulsively.

Conflict Resolution Through Collaboration

Instead of blaming each other, Giver + Giver couples work together to find solutions. Their focus on mutual happiness motivates them to resolve conflicts quickly and amicably.

Focus on Emotional Reassurance

In moments of distress, they provide emotional support rather than criticism. This reassures both partners that they are loved and valued, reducing insecurities and misunderstandings.

Shared Accountability

These couples accept responsibility for their actions and apologize sincerely when necessary. Their willingness to make amends strengthens trust and prevents lingering resentment.

Real-Life Example: The Strength of Mutual Giving

Nisha and Ravi: A Giver + Giver Story Nisha, a compassionate social worker, and Ravi, a dedicated doctor, both lead demanding lives centered on helping others. They met at a charity event where they immediately connected over their shared passion for service.

Their relationship blossomed because they both prioritized giving—not just to the world but also to each other. Whether organizing health camps or volunteering together, their shared mission brought them closer.

When Nisha felt overwhelmed by her work, Ravi supported her emotionally. Similarly, when Ravi faced professional challenges, Nisha was his pillar of strength. Despite their busy lives, they also valued self-care, carving out time to recharge individually and together. This balance allowed them to maintain their energy and continue giving without burnout.

Case Study: Long-Term Success in Giver + Giver Marriages

A study conducted by Dr. John Gottman at the Gottman Institute found that successful marriages often thrive on mutual admiration and emotional support. In one study, couples who actively practiced appreciation and gratitude reported higher levels of satisfaction and longevity in their relationships.

In these marriages, partners demonstrated qualities akin to Giver + Giver dynamics, prioritizing each other's happiness and emotional well-being. They shared a sense of purpose and created rituals of connection—small gestures like morning coffee or handwritten notes—ensuring ongoing emotional intimacy.

How to Nurture a Giver + Giver Relationship

Mutual Support

Actively support each other's personal and professional growth.

Be present during tough times and celebrate achievements together.

Open Communication

Regularly check in with each other to ensure emotional needs are met.

Transparent communication prevents misunderstandings and strengthens trust.

Self-Care

Prioritize self-care to avoid emotional depletion.

Healthy, well-balanced individuals contribute to a stronger partnership.

Shared Values and Goals

Identify a common purpose or set of values.

A shared mission, like helping others or personal growth, solidifies the foundation of your relationship.

Relationship Scenarios and Tips

Giver + Giver Combination

If You Are Single and Looking for a Partner

Look for someone who shares your values of empathy and selflessness.

Focus on mutual emotional availability; avoid relationships where giving is one-sided.

Build self-awareness to understand your own needs and communicate them clearly.

If You Are in Love or Dating

Prioritize open communication to ensure neither partner neglects self-care.

Celebrate small acts of kindness and build rituals of connection.

Be proactive in identifying each other's emotional or physical exhaustion.

If You Are Married

Foster a strong foundation by setting shared goals, like community service or family milestones.

Make time for self-care and mutual relaxation to avoid burnout.

Embrace gratitude and regular affirmations to maintain emotional intimacy.

Conclusion

Giver + Giver relationships embody harmony and balance through their mutual focus on selflessness and care. Rooted in psychological principles such as altruism, secure attachment, and positive reinforcement, these partnerships are not only fulfilling but also resilient. Real-life examples and studies demonstrate that such dynamics foster long-term happiness and emotional stability. By prioritizing communication, self-care, and shared values, Giver + Giver couples can sustain their bond and continue to inspire each other to give, grow, and thrive.

FIVE

CHAPTER 4: GIVER + SEEKER = THE BALANCING ACT

"A Giver and a Seeker can thrive only when balance replaces dependence."

The Initial Harmony: How This Dynamic Works at First

When a Giver and a Seeker first come together, the relationship may appear flawless. The Giver feels fulfilled in their role of providing care, love, and support, while the Seeker enjoys receiving these gifts, finding emotional stability in the Giver's nurturing presence. There is an apparent harmony that makes both partners feel seen and valued.

However, as time goes on, the balance between the Giver and Seeker begins to shift. Initially, there seems to be an equal exchange—one gives, the other receives—but this equilibrium is inherently fragile. The problem begins when the reciprocal nature of the relationship is not maintained. Both parties may unconsciously assume that this initial state of harmony will continue indefinitely, leading to an over-reliance on one side.

The Challenges: When a Giver's Energy Gets Drained

Eventually, the cracks in the relationship start to appear. The Giver, who thrives on providing care, can begin to feel emotionally drained. Their tendency to give without pause or boundaries might lead to burnout, frustration, and a growing sense of resentment. Psychologically, the Giver's sense of self-worth becomes tied to their ability to nurture and support, and when they feel this is unreciprocated, they may begin to question their role in the relationship.

On the Seeker's side, their needs may remain largely unchanged or even increase. They might not recognize that the Giver is reaching a breaking point. Instead, they may take the Giver's constant support for granted, often focusing on their own emotional or material needs without offering much in return. In some cases, the Seeker might feel entitled to the Giver's care, exacerbating the imbalance. Without awareness of the Giver's diminishing energy, the Seeker's expectations grow, further distancing them from the mutual support needed for the relationship to thrive.

What is Not Working

This dynamic begins to unravel when the imbalance between giving and receiving becomes evident. The primary issue is that the Giver's continuous support is not reciprocated in a way that satisfies their emotional needs. The Seeker's emotional growth may stagnate, as they fail to evolve into a giver themselves, maintaining their dependency on the Giver.

The Giver's energy starts to deplete due to the lack of balance. As they withdraw, whether physically or emotionally, the Seeker's sense of abandonment and confusion increases. The relationship loses its vitality when the Giver begins to feel unappreciated, and the Seeker cannot understand the Giver's withdrawal. This disconnect results in the deterioration of the emotional bond.

The Giver may also feel that their needs are not being recognized or valued, which can lead to resentment. They may experience emotional burnout, a common issue when someone gives without boundaries or without receiving support in return. The Seeker, on the other hand, may remain unaware of the Giver's strain, caught in their own emotional needs, which creates a gap in understanding and empathy.

Why This Doesn't Work

The fundamental problem in this dynamic is the lack of reciprocity. Relationships thrive on mutual exchange and understanding. When one party is continuously giving and the other is merely receiving, the bond starts to erode. The Giver feels exhausted, emotionally unfulfilled, and perhaps even resentful, while the Seeker, focused on their own needs, fails to recognize the growing distance between them.

The imbalance is often exacerbated by emotional entitlement, where the Seeker might feel they have the right to demand more from the Giver without giving anything back. This causes frustration for the Giver, who may begin to question their role and sense of self-worth in the relationship. Without this balance, the Giver becomes a source of emotional depletion, and the Seeker becomes a mirror of unaddressed need.

The Psychological Implications

From a psychological standpoint, the failure of the Giver + Seeker dynamic can trigger a range of emotional reactions. The Giver might experience feelings of inadequacy or guilt when they cannot continue giving, while the Seeker may struggle with feelings of rejection or abandonment. The lack of communication and empathy between the two can result in a vicious cycle of emotional strain, ultimately undermining the emotional intimacy that once existed.

Furthermore, this dynamic may prevent both individuals from growing emotionally. The Giver, without learning to set boundaries, may never experience self-care, while the Seeker may remain emotionally stagnant, never learning to give back or take responsibility for their own emotional well-being.

Without change, both individuals are trapped in a cycle where neither is able to evolve, leaving the relationship vulnerable to collapse. The Giver feels overwhelmed and underappreciated, while the Seeker may never fully understand or address the emotional withdrawal of the Giver. Both are stuck in roles that no longer serve the health of the relationship.

Real-Life Example:

Naina and Rohan: A Giver + Seeker Dynamic

Naina, a compassionate and deeply empathetic individual, found herself drawn to Rohan, a charming yet emotionally reserved person. While their relationship started with excitement and promise, their contrasting approaches to love and emotional connection soon began to surface.

The Issue: The Giver's Exhaustion

Naina, the Giver, poured her energy into nurturing Rohan. She constantly anticipated his needs, offering emotional support, encouragement, and even managing responsibilities to ease his stress. On the other hand, Rohan, the Seeker, appreciated Naina's efforts but struggled to reciprocate emotionally. He had grown accustomed to receiving but found it challenging to offer the same level of care.

Over time, Naina began to feel drained. Her attempts to make Rohan feel valued and supported often went unacknowledged, leaving her questioning whether her efforts were truly making a difference. The imbalance caused her to experience emotional burnout, as she felt she was giving far more than she received.

How the Giver Gets Drained

One-Sided Emotional Labor: Naina took on the majority of the emotional responsibilities in the relationship, constantly addressing Rohan's needs without her own being met.

Lack of Reciprocity: While Rohan appreciated Naina's gestures, he rarely initiated acts of care, leaving her feeling undervalued.

Unclear Boundaries: Naina's inability to set boundaries led to her giving beyond her emotional capacity, further exacerbating her fatigue.

Seeker's Dependency: Rohan relied heavily on Naina's emotional support, creating a dynamic where he grew dependent rather than evolving into a more giving partner.

Resolution and Lessons Learned

Recognizing the unsustainable nature of their relationship, Naina and Rohan decided to address their dynamic through open communication and mutual effort.

Setting Boundaries: Naina expressed her need for balance and asked Rohan to contribute more actively to the relationship.

Encouraging Growth: Rohan began working on his emotional availability, practicing small acts of giving and learning to anticipate Naina's needs.

Seeking Support: They attended couples' counseling, which helped them identify underlying patterns and establish healthier dynamics.

Prioritizing Self-Care: Naina made self-care a priority, ensuring she had time to recharge and maintain her emotional well-being.

Key Takeaways for Giver + Seeker Relationships

Boundaries Are Essential: Givers must establish and enforce boundaries to avoid emotional burnout.

Encourage Reciprocity: Seekers should be encouraged to practice giving in small, manageable ways to create a balanced dynamic.

Open Communication: Honest conversations about expectations and needs are crucial to maintaining harmony.

Focus on Growth: Both partners must be willing to grow individually and as a couple to foster a healthy, enduring relationship.

Giver + Seeker Combination

If You Are Single and Looking for a Partner

Be cautious about establishing boundaries early to prevent burnout.

Seek a Seeker who is open to growing emotionally and learning to give back.

Ensure that your giving doesn't become enabling behavior for the Seeker.

If You Are in Love or Dating

Regularly discuss the balance of giving and receiving in the relationship.

Encourage the Seeker to practice small acts of giving, building reciprocity over time.

Avoid resentment by expressing your needs clearly and kindly.

If You Are Married

Ensure that giving doesn't overshadow your own well-being; advocate for shared responsibilities.

Support the Seeker's personal growth to create a more balanced dynamic.

Use structured communication methods to resolve conflicts or misunderstandings.

Conclusion

The Giver + Seeker dynamic, at its core, operates on the idea of mutual exchange. When this balance is disrupted, both parties suffer emotionally. The Seeker's inability to evolve and give back leads to the Giver's exhaustion, creating a disconnection that threatens the relationship's sustainability. Understanding and addressing the imbalance between giving and receiving is crucial to maintaining a healthy, thriving relationship. Without this, the dynamic will eventually deteriorate, leaving both partners emotionally drained and disconnected.

SIX

Chapter 5: Seeker + Seeker = A Shallow Bond

"When two Seekers meet, love becomes a transaction; only giving can deepen the bond."

The Root Cause: Why Seeker + Seeker Relationships Often Fail

When two Seekers come together, the initial spark may seem promising, but the relationship often falters as the true dynamics unfold. Psychologically, the Seeker is someone who is driven by the need to receive—emotional support, validation, or material benefits—rather than the desire to give. In the case of two Seekers, this creates a situation where both partners are more focused on fulfilling their personal needs than on creating a meaningful, balanced connection.

The mutual attraction that brings these two individuals together is often based on the satisfaction of immediate desires—whether emotional, material, or social. Both partners are looking to take, rather than give, which sets the stage for a transactional relationship. This transactional nature is, in many ways, a defense mechanism. From a psychological standpoint, both Seekers may be unconsciously avoiding vulnerability, which is essential for forming deeper emotional bonds. The lack of willingness to emotionally invest in each other limits the potential for true intimacy.

Over time, as these initial needs are met, the relationship begins to show cracks. The satisfaction derived from surface-level exchanges wanes, and the bond fails to deepen. Without emotional vulnerability or selfless giving, the relationship remains superficial, making it difficult for either partner to truly connect. Research on relationship dynamics shows that mutual dependence is vital to long-term stability. Without this, the Seeker + Seeker combination lacks the emotional substance to weather life's challenges, leading to inevitable disillusionment and dissolution.

Materialistic Love: The Pitfalls of Surface-Level Connections

In Seeker + Seeker relationships, the focus often shifts toward materialism or superficial characteristics, which provide immediate gratification but fail to build emotional depth. Psychological studies have shown that while physical attraction and material wealth can serve as powerful initial motivators in romantic relationships, they often fade over time. As the initial allure of wealth, beauty, or social status diminishes, the true nature of the connection—or lack thereof—becomes painfully apparent.

When both partners prioritize surface-level attributes over deeper emotional or spiritual connections, the relationship becomes rooted in material exchanges rather than genuine affection. This often leads to a sense of emptiness and dissatisfaction once the novelty of the material benefits wears off. A study on materialistic relationships found that individuals in such relationships report lower levels of happiness, emotional fulfillment, and long-term satisfaction.

As the relationship progresses, both Seekers may begin to question whether they are truly valued for who they are or merely for the external benefits they offer. The lack of deeper emotional bonding leaves the relationship vulnerable to superficiality, and both individuals may eventually feel as though they are "using" each other to meet their own needs. This materialistic focus, though initially satisfying, becomes unsustainable when the deeper emotional needs of both individuals are ignored.

The Danger of a Lack of Giving in Relationships

Psychologically, relationships require a balance of giving and receiving. Healthy relationships are marked by reciprocal exchange—both partners contribute emotionally, physically, and mentally, nurturing the bond through effort and care. This mutual vulnerability is essential for emotional intimacy and long-term connection. However, in the Seeker + Seeker dynamic, this vital element of giving is often absent.

In such relationships, both individuals are more concerned with receiving than with giving, which creates a cycle of emotional depletion. When both partners are focused solely on fulfilling their own desires, they neglect the emotional needs of the other. Over time, this lack of emotional investment leads to a feeling of emptiness for both parties. The Giver's role, which is critical in sustaining emotional intimacy, is missing, and thus, the relationship can never evolve beyond a shallow connection.

Psychological research highlights that when individuals in a relationship fail to nurture the emotional bond by giving, the relationship stagnates. Even if both partners continue to take from the relationship—whether in the form of attention, affection, or material benefits—they may still feel a deep sense of loneliness or dissatisfaction. The inability to give selflessly leaves both individuals feeling disconnected, ultimately leading to an unsustainable and fragile bond.

Real-Life Example: Seeker + Seeker Dynamic and Its Downfall

Karan and Simran's Story

Karan, a successful businessman, and Simran, a glamorous model, are a classic example of the Seeker + Seeker dynamic. Their initial connection was based on the attraction of material wealth and physical beauty. Karan's financial success was appealing to Simran, while Karan was captivated by Simran's appearance and social status. Their relationship, initially full of excitement, began with an exchange of lavish gifts, luxurious experiences, and public admiration. Both partners seemed to fulfill the other's immediate desires, and they basked in the superficial aspects of their bond.

However, as time passed, cracks began to form in their connection. Karan began to feel that Simran was more interested in his wealth than in him as a person, while Simran started to sense that Karan valued her primarily for her looks and status, rather than for her true self. Neither partner was willing to engage emotionally or give selflessly to the relationship. The focus on material exchanges left little room for emotional investment or mutual care.

This transactional nature of their relationship eventually led to disillusionment. Despite their glamorous lifestyle and public appearances, both Karan and Simran began to feel increasingly empty. They realized they had little to offer each other beyond the material gains they provided. As the excitement of superficial pleasures wore off, they found that their connection lacked the emotional depth needed for a lasting bond. Disheartened by the realization that they had been using each other for personal fulfillment, they ultimately parted ways, each searching for a deeper, more meaningful connection.

Seeker + Seeker Combination

If You Are Single and Looking for a Partner

Focus on self-development before seeking a partner.

Reflect on how to cultivate a more balanced dynamic within the relationship.

Be aware of potential challenges in meeting each other's emotional needs.

If You Are in Love or Dating

Create opportunities for mutual growth, such as shared goals or hobbies.

Invest in professional or personal development to enhance emotional maturity.

Work together to cultivate empathy and understanding within the relationship.

If You Are Married

Work on individual self-improvement to become more giving partners.

Seek external support, such as counseling, to navigate challenges.

Regularly evaluate and adjust the relationship dynamic to foster long-term growth.

Conclusion: The Shallow Nature of Seeker + Seeker Relationships

The Seeker + Seeker dynamic, while initially alluring, is often destined for failure due to the lack of emotional depth and selfless giving. Psychological studies confirm that relationships built on materialism or superficial attraction are unlikely to endure in the long term. Without the willingness to give—emotionally, physically, or mentally—the relationship remains transactional, leaving both individuals feeling unsatisfied and unfulfilled.

The root cause of this failure lies in the inability of both partners to engage in reciprocal emotional exchanges that nurture the bond. The absence of mutual vulnerability and the focus on receiving rather than giving create an unsustainable relationship, leading to inevitable disillusionment and emotional emptiness. For a Seeker + Seeker relationship to thrive, both partners must be willing to give selflessly, breaking free from the cycle of materialism and surface-level connections. Without this shift, the relationship is bound to remain shallow and ultimately fall apart.

SEVEN

Chapter 6: Finding Balance in Love

"Balance in love is not about perfection, but about two souls learning to give and receive in harmony."

Self-Reflection: Are You a Giver or a Seeker?

Understanding your role in relationships is essential to achieving balance. People often find themselves gravitating towards one of two primary roles: the Giver or the Seeker. While neither role is inherently negative, imbalance can lead to dissatisfaction and conflict. Identifying your tendencies can help you navigate love with greater awareness and harmony.

Are You a Giver?

Givers often derive fulfillment from nurturing and supporting others. They find joy in acts of kindness and selflessness but may sometimes neglect their own needs. While giving is a beautiful trait, overgiving without reciprocity can lead to emotional exhaustion and resentment.

Questions to consider:

Do you feel most fulfilled when you make others happy?

Do you often prioritize others' needs over your own?

Do you sometimes feel drained or unappreciated after giving too much without receiving in return?

Are You a Seeker?

Seekers tend to look outward for emotional fulfillment. They often rely on others to meet their emotional needs and may struggle to give without expecting something in return. Seekers crave attention, love, and validation, which can create imbalance if not balanced with giving.

Questions to consider:

Do you often look to others to fulfill your emotional needs?

Do you feel unfulfilled when you don't receive enough attention or affection?

Do you find yourself constantly seeking more from your partner?

By reflecting on these questions, you can identify your tendencies and work towards a healthier dynamic in your relationships.

Steps for Seekers to Learn the Art of Giving

Seekers can enhance their relationships by cultivating the ability to give selflessly. True emotional fulfillment often arises from acts of giving without expectation. When Seekers practice empathy and prioritize others' needs, they can foster stronger and more meaningful connections.

Practical Steps for Seekers:

Practice Empathy: Cultivate the ability to step into someone else's shoes. Being present for others, listening deeply, and offering emotional support can strengthen bonds and demonstrate care.

Example: Instead of focusing on how your partner's actions affect you, try to understand their perspective and feelings.

Give Without Expectation: Shift your mindset to offer without expecting anything in return. This can create a more authentic and generous relationship dynamic.

Example: Surprise your partner with a thoughtful gesture without waiting for acknowledgment or reciprocation.

Set Healthy Boundaries: Giving does not mean depleting yourself. Protect your energy and ensure that your giving is sustainable.

Example: If you feel overwhelmed, communicate your limits rather than stretching yourself too thin.

Invest in Self-Care: A well-cared-for self is better equipped to give. Prioritize your emotional and physical health to avoid burnout.

Example: Dedicate time to hobbies, rest, or activities that rejuvenate you.

Be a Listener: Sometimes, the most powerful act of giving is simply listening. By being attentive and present, you show your partner that their thoughts and feelings matter.

Example: During conversations, resist the urge to interject and focus on truly understanding what your partner is expressing.

How Givers Can Avoid Burnout and Seek Reciprocity

While giving is a noble quality, Givers often neglect their own needs, leading to emotional exhaustion. To maintain balance, Givers must learn to receive love and care from others, ensuring that their relationships are mutually fulfilling.

Strategies for Givers:

Recognize Your Limits: Understand that it's okay to say "no" when necessary. Setting boundaries ensures that you can give without compromising your well-being.

Example: Politely decline a request if you feel overwhelmed and offer to help at a later time.

Allow Others to Give: Accepting support is not a sign of weakness. Letting your partner give back fosters deeper connection and balance.

Example: If your partner offers to take care of something for you, graciously accept instead of insisting on doing it yourself.

Practice Self-Care: Regularly engage in activities that recharge your energy and bring you joy.

Example: Spend an afternoon reading, meditating, or engaging in a hobby you love.

Ask for Help: Reach out for support when needed. Allowing others to contribute can strengthen relationships.

Example: Share your feelings with your partner and let them know how they can support you.

Create Time for Yourself: Ensure you have moments of solitude for reflection and relaxation.

Example: Schedule regular "me time" to unwind and recharge.

How to Build Balanced, Healthy Relationships

Achieving balance in love requires mutual effort and understanding. When both partners are committed to growth and reciprocity, relationships can thrive.

Tips for Balanced Relationships:

Open Communication: Share your needs, desires, and boundaries with your partner regularly. Honest communication fosters trust and understanding.

Example: Have a weekly check-in where you both discuss your feelings and any concerns.

Mutual Giving: Ensure that both partners contribute to the relationship. A flow of love and respect creates a stronger bond.

Example: Take turns planning date nights or surprising each other with small gestures of love.

Practice Gratitude: Regularly express appreciation for your partner's efforts. Gratitude strengthens emotional connection.

Example: Write a heartfelt note or verbally acknowledge something your partner did that you're thankful for.

Be Patient: Balance takes time to achieve. Trust the process and give each other room to grow.

Example: If your partner struggles with a habit, encourage their progress rather than expecting immediate change.

Support Each Other's Growth: Encourage personal and emotional development, fostering mutual respect and understanding.

Example: Celebrate your partner's achievements and be their cheerleader in pursuing their goals.

EIGHT

Chapter 7: The Key to Sustainability: Mutual Giving

"Sustainability in love lies in mutual giving, where both partners thrive through shared care."

The Power of Mutual Giving and the Long-Term Fulfillment It Brings:

At the core of every thriving relationship lies the principle of mutual giving. It is the dance of love, where both partners actively invest in each other's happiness, well-being, and growth. Mutual giving transcends mere transactions; it is about creating a rhythm of reciprocity that strengthens the foundation of love, trust, and connection.

When two individuals commit to equally contributing to the relationship, they build a shared reservoir of emotional wealth. This reciprocity fosters unity, mutual respect, and the assurance that both are equally invested in the bond. Unlike one-sided dynamics, where imbalance leads to resentment or emotional depletion, mutual giving ensures that both partners feel valued, cherished, and supported.

Relationships that embody mutual giving are marked by resilience and harmony. Each partner becomes attuned to the other's needs, offering love and care not out of obligation but from a genuine desire to nurture the bond. Over time, this balance creates a relationship that is both fulfilling and sustainable, where growth happens together, not apart.

Creating and Maintaining a Healthy, Balanced Dynamic

Sustaining mutual giving requires intentionality and commitment. While love may spark spontaneously, its endurance depends on conscious effort from both partners. Here are practical ways to cultivate and maintain a balanced dynamic in your relationship:

Be Present and Attentive

Show your partner that you are emotionally available. Pay attention to their words, actions, and unspoken needs. Sometimes, the most meaningful gift is your undivided presence.

Communicate Your Needs

Healthy relationships thrive on open communication. Share your feelings and needs honestly, and encourage your partner to do the same. Transparency eliminates guesswork and ensures both partners feel understood.

Express Gratitude

A simple "thank you" can go a long way in reinforcing the bond. Acknowledge the little things your partner does, whether it's making you coffee in the morning or offering emotional support after a tough day. Gratitude fosters positivity and strengthens mutual respect.

Celebrate Each Other's Successes

Be your partner's biggest cheerleader. Celebrate their achievements, big or small, with genuine enthusiasm. This shared joy fosters a sense of partnership and strengthens your connection.

Maintain Emotional Balance

Both partners must prioritize emotional well-being. Avoid situations where one partner bears the brunt of emotional labor. Instead, create an environment where both can share burdens and joys equally.

Offer Support without Overwhelming

Support should be meaningful and measured. Avoid the temptation to overextend yourself, as it can lead to burnout. Strive to help your partner while maintaining your own well-being.

Create a Safe Space for Vulnerability

True intimacy stems from vulnerability. Foster an atmosphere where both partners feel safe to express their fears, dreams, and insecurities without judgment.

Real-Life Example: A Balanced Relationship in Practice

Consider the story of Priya and Aarav, a couple who exemplify mutual giving. Priya is a writer who often struggles with self-doubt, while Aarav, a marketing professional, has a demanding job. During a period when Priya was working on a book, Aarav stepped in to manage household chores, giving her the space to focus on her writing.

Later, when Aarav faced stress at work, Priya reciprocated by being his emotional anchor, offering encouragement and ensuring he had time to unwind. Their relationship didn't operate on a ledger of who did more, but on the understanding that they were partners in every sense, balancing each other's needs naturally.

This ebb and flow of support allowed their relationship to thrive. Both felt seen, appreciated, and loved, which strengthened their bond over time.

How to Sustain the Love Equation

Sustaining mutual giving is an ongoing journey. Relationships require nurturing, and the key lies in consistent effort from both partners. Here are steps to sustain this delicate balance:

Regular Check-Ins

Schedule time to reflect on your relationship. Ask each other, "How are we doing?" or "What can I do better?" These conversations allow you to address imbalances early and realign as needed.

Prioritize Quality Time

In the hustle of daily life, it's easy to neglect your partner. Prioritize time together to reconnect, whether through a date night, shared hobby, or a simple walk.

Be Open to Feedback

Accept constructive feedback from your partner with grace. Mutual giving includes the willingness to adapt and improve for the betterment of the relationship.

Nurture Individual Growth

A strong relationship consists of two individuals who are growing and evolving. Encourage your partner's personal aspirations while pursuing your own. When both partners thrive individually, the relationship benefits collectively.

Reaffirm Your Commitment

Small gestures of love, like a handwritten note or a surprise gift, can reaffirm your dedication to each other. These acts show that you value the relationship and are invested in its future.

The Essence of Mutual Giving

In a world where relationships often falter under the weight of unmet expectations, mutual giving emerges as the cornerstone of lasting love. It's a reminder that love isn't just about taking or sacrificing—it's about creating a partnership where both individuals give and receive in harmony.

By embracing mutual giving, you lay the foundation for a relationship that doesn't just survive but thrives. You create a bond that is resilient, fulfilling, and deeply rooted in trust and respect. This is the key to sustainability in love—a dynamic that ensures both partners flourish together, hand in hand.

NINE

Chapter 8: Love Beyond Labels

"True love transcends roles and labels, flourishing in its fluidity and freedom."

The Constraints of Labels

Labels like "Giver," "Seeker," "Provider," or "Receiver" are often assigned to define roles within relationships. While they can provide clarity, they also impose limitations, confining individuals to predefined identities that may not reflect the full scope of their emotional depth or potential.

A Giver, for example, might feel pressured to constantly provide, while a Receiver might feel guilty for accepting care without reciprocation. These labels can become barriers, preventing partners from truly connecting and adapting to each other's needs as circumstances evolve.

Love transcends these labels. It thrives in an environment of fluidity, where both partners are free to shift roles based on their growth, needs, and the demands of the relationship. By letting go of these constraints, relationships can evolve into more dynamic and fulfilling connections.

Letting Go of Labels: Embracing the Fluid Nature of Relationships

The essence of love lies in its ability to adapt and flow. When partners relinquish rigid roles, they create space for vulnerability, openness, and authenticity. Here's how embracing fluidity can transform relationships:

Breaking Free from Fixed Roles

In a healthy relationship, there's no permanent Giver or Seeker. Partners should feel empowered to switch roles as circumstances dictate. For example, one partner might take on the role of a provider during a challenging phase, only to later rely on their partner for emotional support when their own difficulties arise.

Encouraging Vulnerability

Fluid roles allow both partners to be vulnerable without fear of judgment. A traditionally strong and independent partner can admit moments of weakness, while a partner who typically seeks guidance can step into a leadership role when needed.

Strengthening Empathy

Letting go of labels fosters empathy, as both individuals learn to experience and understand each other's perspectives. This mutual understanding strengthens the bond, creating a partnership rooted in compassion and shared humanity.

The Evolution of Givers and Seekers in Love

Relationships are dynamic, evolving with the growth of each individual. The roles of Giver and Seeker are not fixed; they shift as partners mature and navigate life's changes.

Growth through Experience

A Seeker, often perceived as someone reliant on care and guidance, may gradually evolve into a Giver as they gain confidence, wisdom, and emotional stability. Conversely, a Giver, who may be seen as a source of strength and support, might find themselves in a position of seeking care during times of vulnerability.

The Balance of Roles

The beauty of a fluid relationship lies in its balance. Partners intuitively adjust to meet each other's needs, creating a cycle of giving and receiving that fosters long-term fulfillment. This balance is not always equal at every moment but should even out over time.

Adapting to Life's Seasons

Life is unpredictable, and relationships must adapt to its changing seasons. Whether it's supporting a partner through a career transition, illness, or personal crisis, the ability to shift roles strengthens the partnership and ensures its resilience.

Personal Growth and Evolution in a Relationship

For a relationship to thrive, individual growth is essential. Each partner must prioritize their personal evolution, not as a means of drifting apart, but as a way of enhancing the relationship.

Supporting Individual Journeys

Encouraging your partner's personal growth shows respect for their individuality. This could involve supporting them in pursuing a new career, learning a skill, or exploring their passions.

Embracing Change

Change is inevitable, and personal growth often involves redefining one's identity. A partner's willingness to adapt and embrace these changes fosters a relationship that evolves alongside them.

Avoiding Stagnation

When one partner grows while the other remains stagnant, the relationship can feel unbalanced. Both individuals must strive for self-improvement, ensuring the partnership continues to inspire and fulfill.

Growth Together

Personal growth doesn't mean neglecting the relationship; rather, it enriches it. Partners who grow individually bring new perspectives, energy, and strength to the relationship, keeping it vibrant and dynamic.

Love Beyond Labels

True love transcends societal norms and predefined roles. It's about connecting with a partner on a human level, embracing their flaws, celebrating their growth, and standing by them in every phase of life. By letting go of labels, couples can experience love in its purest form—free, fluid, and ever-evolving.

This approach fosters a partnership where both individuals feel valued, respected, and loved not for their roles but for who they are. Love beyond labels is not just a concept; it's a practice that builds relationships capable of withstanding the tests of time and change.

TEN

Conclusion: The Future of Love and Relationships

"The future of love lies in balance, understanding, and the courage to grow together."

Unlocking the Secrets of Lasting Love

As we reflect on the journey through the intricacies of love and relationships, one message stands out clearly: lasting love is a blend of balance, empathy, and reciprocity. By delving into the dynamics of Givers and Seekers, we've uncovered the fundamental principles that sustain healthy, fulfilling relationships.

Key Lessons Learned:

Mutual Giving and Receiving: The balance of giving and receiving is crucial to maintaining emotional well-being and trust within a relationship. Both partners must actively participate to nurture the bond.

Awareness of Roles: Recognizing when to step into the roles of Giver or Seeker ensures that neither partner feels overburdened or neglected.

Growth through Balance: Lasting love requires equilibrium where both partners feel valued, supported, and free to grow individually and together.

An imbalance in these roles often leads to dissatisfaction, creating tension and emotional exhaustion. The true essence of love lies in understanding, adapting, and evolving with one another.

The Importance of Balance, Giving, and Understanding

At the heart of every successful relationship lies balance. It is neither about relentless sacrifice nor selfish fulfillment but about creating harmony where both individuals thrive.

Selfless yet Self-Aware Giving: While giving is an integral part of love, it should never come at the expense of one's own identity or well-being. A sustainable relationship requires that each partner be whole within themselves, giving from a place of abundance rather than depletion.

The Willingness to Receive: Receiving love is just as important as giving it. By being open to receiving care and support, partners build trust and foster vulnerability, creating a safe space for deeper emotional intimacy.

Adapting to Change: Love is not static; it evolves as individuals and their circumstances change. Understanding and accommodating these shifts is vital for maintaining connection and ensuring long-term growth.

Mutual Respect and Trust: These are the pillars that support the structure of any relationship. Without respect and trust, the balance between giving and receiving falters, leading to instability.

Love is a living, breathing entity that requires ongoing attention and care. It flourishes in an environment of mutual understanding, where both partners are invested in each other's well-being.

A Call to Action: Reflect and Grow

As we stand at the crossroads of understanding and practice, I encourage you to take a moment to reflect on your relationships:

Are you giving enough, or are you holding back out of fear or past experiences?

Are you open to receiving love and support without guilt or hesitation?

Are your relationships balanced, or do they lean too heavily on one partner?

Take this opportunity to assess your role in your relationships. Whether you identify as a Giver or a Seeker, the goal is to create harmony by embracing fluidity and adaptability. True love demands that both individuals commit to personal growth, evolving together while respecting each other's individuality.

Embrace the challenge of nurturing your relationships—not only with others but also with yourself. By fostering self-awareness and practicing mutual care, you can create connections that are both profound and enduring.

A Vision for the Future

The future of love lies in breaking free from outdated notions and rigid roles. Love isn't just a label or a fleeting emotion; it's a continuous journey of balance, respect, and shared growth. Together, let us reimagine love as a dynamic force—one that unites individuals in harmony and builds a foundation for a compassionate and connected world.

Final Quote

"Love is the harmony of two souls growing together, giving without losing, and seeking without draining—an endless journey of balance, freedom, and connection."

Dilip Chakravarthy

www.ingramcontent.com/pod-product-compliance
Lightning Source LLC
LaVergne TN
LVHW041231150826
845673LV00008B/2349